THE RULE

IN

MINOT'S CASE

AGAIN:

AS RESTATED WITH VARIATIONS BY THE SUPREME JUDICIAL COURT OF MASSACHUSETTS.

"As to the distinction between stock and money — that is too thin." — LORD ELDON, in *Paris* v. *Paris*.

"Not a solid distinction." — LORD ELDON in *Barclay* v. *Wainwright*.

BY A LAYMAN.

NEW YORK:
G. P. PUTNAM AND SONS,
ASSOCIATION BUILDING, 4TH AVENUE AND 23D STREET.
1871.

THE

RULE IN MINOT'S CASE AGAIN.

Not long since I submitted, to whom it might concern, a layman's review of a law recently enacted by the Supreme Judicial Court of Massachusetts. This law was modestly described by the court as a simple rule, laying down a plain principle to which trustees were entitled, to guide them in the discharge of their duties. After its promulgation there were to be no more doubting trustees. The simple rule and the plain principle, enounced in the most crisp and laconic language, were not only to relieve the consciences of trustees forever, but to lighten the onerous labors of the judiciary. *Cestuis que trust* were to pocket all cash dividends, " however large," and remainder-men were to be the happy recipients of all stock dividends, "however made." This was the whole of it. There was to be no further need of going behind the action of directors, or investigating the concerns of corporations. *Redeunt Saturnia regna.* Halcyon days were in store for all of us, — a state of things not unlike that which prevailed when Robin Hood judged and legislated for Sherwood Forest, and with a rustic fondness for plain principles administered affairs upon

"The good old rule, . . . the simple plan, —
That they should take who have the power,
And they should keep who can."

By the circumstances mentioned in the Review my attention had been called to the *Rule in Minot's case*, and to the decision in which the rule was announced. I studied the decision with great care, and failed to see the *rule* it expounded in the rosy aspect which it presented to the court. I regarded it as impossible law, and as a fruitful source of injustice; and from a layman's point of view I endeavored to assign the reasons for my conclusions. These were printed in a pamphlet, copies of which were sent to the judges and officers of the Supreme Court, to the several public libraries, to a few members of the profession, and to several journals in different parts of the State.

Not many days after this publication I was breakfasting at the Club, when Jeems handed me the morning paper. It was the "Daily Advertiser," and my eye was arrested at once by the following paragraph, in a review of volume 101 of the "Massachusetts Reports:"

> "An interesting ruling concerning dividends payable upon trust-funds is to be found in *Daland* v. *Williams*, p. 571. When the cause of *Minot* vs. *Paine* (99 Mass. 101) was decided, a few years since, it caused a good deal of comment and excitement. It laid down the rule regarding stock dividends, that they were not payable to the person who was beneficiary of the trust for life, but were to be added to the capital for the benefit of the persons finally entitled to take the principal in fee. Trustees had, theretofore, been very apt to pursue the contrary course. It is only a short time since a pamphlet, containing severe strictures upon that decision, has been privately circulated among the legal fraternity. *But the court in this later cause have gone even a step further than they went in* Minot *vs.* Paine, *and in the same direction.*"

I read no further. Swallowing my light repast, in the manner in which General Scott dispatched the historical plate of soup, I hurried to my lawyer's with the paper in my hand, and the fatal words "*further in the same direction*" on my lips.

My friend is early at his office, and I broke in upon him rather abruptly with a "Look there." I observed, as he ran his eye over the paragraph, "We must have a new will, I'm afraid. In providing for my nephew Richard, you only went as far as the court had gone *then*, but now the court has gone FURTHER! We must keep up with the court, and cover all their new ground as fast as they make it. If they've gone further, we must go further too."

His eye twinkling with malicious humor, — I don't think it was the prospect of another fee that inspired it, — my legal friend knocked the ashes from his cigar and motioned me to a seat. Taking from his safe a tin box which contained a file of my papers, he withdrew the will to which I referred, and hastily examined it.

"It's my nephew Richard's interest that I'm anxious about," I remarked, as he opened the new volume of Reports and turned to the opinion of the court in the case of *Daland* v. *Williams*.

"It won't be necessary to make a new will, as I see," my friend suggested after a moment's reflection. "You can add a codicil, providing that all your dividends shall go to your nephew Richard, whether they are made 'in the usual manner or in an unusual manner.' I think this will make it all safe for the present, and from time to time you can step in and add such codicils as may be called for by the new decisions."

"But pray tell me," I observed somewhat shyly, "what does the writer mean by saying that the cause of *Minot* v. *Paine*, when it was decided, caused a good deal of 'comment and excitement'?"

"He means among the profession."

"But why didn't the profession say something about it?" I inquired.

"O, they did — among themselves, with their legs under the mahogany, and no judges present — say at Parker's, after an adjournment of court, or when they were closeted in a consultation. Then they 'd blaze away; but in court it would always be 'Your Honors' very able and conclusive opinion in *Minot* v. *Paine*.'"

"Then it was a sort of heat-lightning 'comment and excitement,' I suppose."

"That's it, exactly. The judges believe to this day that there is not a member of the bar within their jurisdiction who does not regard the decision in *Minot* v. *Paine* as the perfection of reason. In fact, if there is one of their judgments which in *their* judgment is a little more the perfection of reason than any other it is this very one."

"But about trustees; — the 'Advertiser' says that trustees, before *Minot* v. *Paine*, were very apt to pay over stock dividends to the beneficiaries of the income."

"Certainly. Why not? Testators made no difference between stock and cash dividends, why should trustees? I never knew a case, in old times, in which a trustee withheld a dividend from his *cestui que trust* on the ground of its being made in an unusual manner, or on the ground of its being made in an unusual scrip; — they treated scrip and greenbacks in the same way."

"But the court, I understand, don't like the 'manner' in which this dividend is made in Daland's case. But do they regard manner as more important than 'matters,' which they said they could not investigate with accuracy?"

"Surely, my dear friend, surely. Matters they will

not investigate, — they've said so several times. But the manner of doing a thing, my dear fellow, the *manner*, is well worth looking into, and they are perfectly capable of investigating it with entire accuracy. The court, sir, are judicial Turveydrops, every man of them. They will look into a dividend to see if it is paid in a proper manner; and if it is not paid in a proper and becoming manner, they will brand it as capital, and throw it into the *mortmain* of trusteeship. That's all right, sir. There's no knowing how directors might do things, if we did not keep a strict watch on their manners."

"But they said a stock dividend was capital, *however* it was made, didn't they?"

"Certainly. You can't make a dividend of stock, it's all capital, and no matter what the manner of dividend may be it continues to be capital. But with cash it is different. Divide that in the usual way, and it's income. Divide in an unusual way, and it's capital. Now there is no way, however unusual, in which you can divide stock to make anything but capital of it. The question of *manner* does not arise in regard to stock dividends."

"And is this law?" I asked reverentially.

"Law?" replied my friend; "certainly, 'Crowner's quest law!'"

With this our conversation terminated, and my will being duly adapted by a codicil to the new version of the *Rule in Minot's case*, the subject was dismissed from my thoughts, till my interest in it was revived by a mere accident. Lounging in a public library, I noticed on the table the April number of the "American Law Review," and examining its contents, ascertained that my unprofessional effort had inspired a notice which it answers my purposes to copy verbatim: —

"*Common Sense* versus *Judicial Legislation;* being the Review of a Law recently enacted by the Supreme Court of Massachusetts. By a Layman. New York: G. P. Putnam and Sons. 1871. Pamphlet.

"This pamphlet is a criticism of the case of *Minot* v. *Paine*, 99 Mass. 101, in which the Supreme Court of Massachusetts decided that stock dividends were capital, and not income of a trust fund. It begins in this amusing way: —

"'Not long since I had occasion to consult a lawyer in regard to making my will. I have not much to devise, but among my assets were a few shares of stock in a railroad. These I decided to put into the hands of trustees, with instructions to pay the "whole income" thereof during his life-time to Richard Roe, and transfer the shares on his decease to John Doe.

"'My professional adviser rather startled me by suggesting that the words "whole income" would not carry out my intentions with regard to my nephew Richard, if I wished him to enjoy all the earnings and profits divided by the corporation. Whereupon, thinking to clinch the matter, I replied "Well, add the words 'and all lawful dividends.'"

"'My adviser shook his head. "'Whole income and all lawful dividends' would seem pretty strong," said he, "to the uninitiated, but we lawyers know better."

"'"Then add 'of every name and nature.'" Still my adviser was not content, nor was he satisfied till the clause read: "Whole income and all lawful dividends, whether the same be made in stock, scrip, or cash, and whether the same be styled capital by the Supreme Court of Massachusetts, or otherwise."'

"The writer is evidently possessed of a knowledge of the rudiments of law, although he announces himself as a layman on the title-page. His *brochure* is, on the whole, of no particular value, since the objections which it urges against the decision must be quite patent to all save the laity, and the 'common sense' view of *Minot* v. *Paine*, is not likely to influence the perverted minds of the chief justice and his associates in the decision of future cases. We understand, however, that considerations of a legal character have already induced them to modify the short and simple rule laid down in *Minot* v. *Paine* in decisions not yet reported."

The critic finds my way of beginning "amusing," but he does not seem to be so much entertained by my way of concluding. He admits that even a layman may possess a knowledge of the rudiments of law, but pronounces his *brochure* on the whole of "no particular value." If he had stopped here, he might have had it all his own way; and the layman would have considered himself duly extinguished. But he goes on to assign his reasons for the faith that is in him. Now when a critic, be he a reporter, or a young attorney, or any other officer of a court, undertakes or volunteers in defence of an unfortunate decision of the judges, he should do as a clever lawyer does when he has a bad case, — confine himself, as far as possible, to abuse of the opposing counsel. It is always the safest way. The sneer at "rudiments," and the sentence of "no particular value" are capital; and the critic might well have plumed himself on achieving them. But as to his defence of the judges, if he manages his next case in the Municipal Court with no more discretion, his client will have to look through a grating for the full term assigned by the law for his offence.

The *brochure*, forsooth, is of "no particular value," because the objections it urges against the decision must be "quite patent to all save the laity." This is a very liberal saving. Unless Massachusetts is worse ridden by the profession than she ought to be, the lay people must outnumber the lawyers by an hundred to one; and it was valuable to these laymen to know that objections existed of a grave character to an important law, which were "patent" to the bench and the bar, but in regard to which the bench and the bar had preserved a discreet and profitable silence. It was the writer's intention to make the objections "patent" to the most limited knowledge and the most humble capacity, and to this benevolent endeavor the

2

reviewer ought to be the last person to take exception.

But if the objections to *Minot* v. *Paine* are patent, the critic does not venture to deny that they are very grave and well-founded objections. To charge and to demonstrate that the Supreme Court of Massachusetts, in the year 1868, have established the doctrine of *Brander* v. *Brander*, under the pretence of repudiating it, is certainly no light objection, if it is true; and to this day no one has denied that such is the effect of *Minot* v. *Paine*. To charge and to demonstrate that in his anxiety to recommend obsolete doctrines to the profession, the Chief Justice had misunderstood the results of the two New York cases, and had described them as coinciding with his views when they were in every respect diametrically opposed to them, is to raise an objection that no friend of the court should be disposed to dismiss as a patent one to all save the laity. To charge and to demonstrate that *Minot* v. *Paine* lays down a simple rule containing two propositions, both of which unqualified are on their face untenable and absurd, raises an objection so serious, that a lawyer who admits its patency should not compromise himself by undervaluing its importance.

But another reason that renders the *brochure* of "no particular value," is that the "perverted minds" of the six judges are not likely to be influenced by a "common-sense" view of their decision. The *innuendo* here is that the decision in *Minot* v. *Paine* is all right, in spite of the objections which are patent to all save the laity. Or does the critic mean that the court are inaccessible to the suggestions of common-sense views, and that such suggestions ought not to influence the court? To admit that the objections exist, that they are obvious, and yet to assert that they are not likely to have any influence on the court, because they are the suggestions of a layman, is to assume that only the very few individuals bred to the profession have the right to formulate an objection to a judicial decision which the court can with propriety consider. The layman avers that the *Rule in Minot's Case* is a local error, and that although it has the force of law in Massachusetts, it is not law. If this is believed to be so, and good reasons are given for the belief, then the minds of the court are "perverted" if they refuse to listen to them, on the ground that a layman has no rights in the premises which the court is "bound to respect."

But though the judges will refuse to be influenced by "common sense," the reviewer understands (from the same source perhaps) that "considerations of a *legal character* have already induced them to modify the short and simple rule laid down in *Minot* v. *Paine*, *in decisions not yet reported.*" It is idle to talk about "modifying" the *rule in Minot's case.* When it is modified sufficiently to take all out of it that is not law, there will be nothing left. We shall be duly grateful for every modification of this rule that takes something away from it; but we can't help thinking with the link-boy to whom Pope refused a penny, with his usual exclamation of "God mend me!" "Mend *you!* It would be easier to make a new one."

It is to be borne in mind that this review is written in the interest of the judges, and in rebuke of the lay scribbler who undertakes to criticize their decision. It is a defence of the court. It says, no doubt, the best that can be said for *Minot* v. *Paine;* and that best is as near a *cognovit* as can well be. It is a confession and avoidance, *minus* the avoidance.

But the court have already modified their short and simple rule, and the promise of future modification in unreported cases makes it worth while to examine more particularly the modification that has already been accomplished. The simple rule, then, had not been law for a twelvemonth, when certain trustees who were to be guided by it could not see their way clear without an application to the court for its construction. One would think it clear to the humblest comprehension. It is so positively and distinctly expressed that the most subtle caviller can hardly place upon it two interpretations.

But alas for simplicity, antithesis, and laconics! They would not stand the first shock. In March, 1869, Mr. Henry T. Daland and others, trustees, filed a bill in equity against the four daughters of the late Tucker Daland, of Salem, who were the beneficiaries under his will of the annual income (among other things) of fifty-six shares of stock in the Hill Manufacturing Company, a corporation established under the laws of Maine at Lewiston in that State. Its capital stock was $700,000, divided into 7,000 shares of the par value of $100. The semi-annual dividends were paid over without diminution to the daughters down to the time of the enactment of the new law by the Supreme Judicial Court of Massachusetts. But on the 16th of January, 1869, the corporation voted to increase their capital to $1,000,000, by issuing 3,000 shares of new stock, at its par value of $100 each. They also declared a DIVIDEND of forty per cent., and authorized the treasurer to receive that dividend in payment for 2,800 shares of the company, and to sell the remaining 200 shares, and to issue certificates of stock to all the purchasers. It was agreed among the parties that the profits divided had been earned and invested in property; and that the corporation would have divided stock instead of cash, had it not been that the laws of Maine do not allow stock-dividends to be made by manufacturing companies. Under these circumstances the plain principle of the court for the guidance of the trustees only furnished light enough to guide them straight to the doors of the court-house for further information. The four daughters of the testator could do nothing but follow them, though they had been judicially told that they ought not to be subjected to any such expense as is involved in the investigation of the doings of directors and the concerns of corporations, especially if they are "out of our jurisdiction."

Their counsel appeared, bold as a lion, before the bench. He held up the broad shield of the new law. "This dividend," said Mr. Hutchins, "is a cash dividend in express terms, behind which terms the court will not go; and is therefore to be treated as income within the rule in *Minot* v. *Paine.*" Certainly. If there were ever an *argumentum ad hominem*, here it is. "A simple rule," said the court, "is to regard cash dividends, however large, as income." "It would be practically unwise," they added, "for courts to go behind the action of the company and attempt to ascertain how they came by the funds out of which they declare either cash or stock dividends." How could Mr. Hutchins have imagined that the court, after the modest declaration of their inability to "investigate such matters with accuracy," would undertake to investigate them at all? But courts have counsel at an advantage. They not only make laws, but they construe them; or to state it with a variation, they not only construe laws, but they make them. The court were equal to the occasion. Hear what the court said to Mr. Hutchins and the four daughters of the testator, by the mouth of the Chief Justice: —

"The case of *Minot* v. *Paine*, 99 Mass. R. 101, states a plain rule for the guidance of trustees in respect to dividends made in the usual manner. Cash dividends are to be regarded as income, and stock dividends as principal."

One might well suppose that six gentlemen on a bench — or off a bench as for that — who had stated a simple rule in 1868, would have been able to restate it with entire accuracy in 1869. We like a strain in Der Freischutz, with variations, sometimes, but we like to take a rule of law pure and simple, the same yesterday and to-morrow. At all events, we like to see a court face its own music. It is not true that *Minot* v. *Paine* lays down its plain rule for the guidance of trustees "in respect to dividends made *in the usual manner*." We are not even left to infer that it is confined to such dividends. Such an idea is expressly excluded in terms, with regard to a large class of dividends. The rule is thus announced in 1868: "A simple rule is, to regard cash dividends, however large, as income; and stock dividends, HOWEVER MADE, as capital." This is the *Rule in Minot's case.* And is such a marvelously "jinglesome" rule to have all the ring taken out of it the very first time it is applied? Do away with the "howevers," and you do away with all the balance of words and the phraseological antithesis that made the Chief Justice and his colleagues imagine that it was law, in the first instance. To dislocate the members of such a rule is an absolute barbarism; and yet dislocated they are, beyond remedy. "However made" is henceforth to be treated as a repealed clause of the *Rule in Minot's case.* "However large" will follow in the natural course of things. It has had a severe side-blow; it is repealed by implication, by its omission in the new version, but it still survives.

And what next?

"But in the present case the manner of making the dividend was unusual, and a question has arisen as to what its character really is."

Now it is odd enough that courts and trustees who cannot be called upon to investigate "matters" connected with the doings of corporations, or to "go behind the action of the company and attempt to ascertain how they came by the funds" they divide, should volunteer to investigate the manner in which they make their dividends. How they get their funds is no trustee's business, and no court's business, but the mode of dividing them is to be strictly an usual mode, or it will be overhauled. The manner of the dividend, and the character of the dividend are both to be inquired into, and a dividend is to have no standing in Judge Chapman's court until it is able to establish a good character, and an unexceptionable manner. Failing this, it is liable to be placed in permanent close imprisonment on a general suspicion of being no better than it should be. But let us see how the court examines the question of manner and character in the present case:—

"In making it, the first step of the directors was to increase their capital stock to $1,000,000, by creating 3,000 shares of new stock at its par value of $100 each. They then declared a dividend of forty per cent., and voted that the treasurer be authorized to receive said dividend in payment for 2,800 shares of the stock, and issue certificates for the dividend."

Follow this insidious and unprincipled performance with the light thrown on it by the dark-lantern of the court. Unwind the threads of this tortuous conspiracy by which a cabal of directors seek thus to repay the money they had borrowed to whom it might concern. Not contented with making $280,000 of net earnings, and investing it in property, they make a first step — that fatal *premier pas qui coûte* — toward having that money put into a representative scrip, or stock representative, of 3,000 shares at $100 each. These shares, the subject of this wicked first step, thus became *net earnings lawfully represented.* "*Then,*" — follow with due reflection the solemn and august development of this conspiracy, — "*then* they declared a dividend of forty per cent.!" This was the second step. You may fail to see its enormity, but that will duly appear no doubt at the next flash of the dark-lantern. Step the third, was to vote authority to the treasurer to receive the money thus voted in exchange for 2,800 shares of the corporation stock *at par*, which would be the precise amount of $280,000 net earnings which the directors, as honest men, felt bound to divide. The residue of the stock they ordered to be sold for the benefit of the corporation, — and this was step the fourth. But I am anticipating. Listen to the court: —

"The balance of the new stock, being 200 shares, they voted to sell. The stock which the shareholders were thus authorized to take, was worth $163 per share. Although there was an implied option that any stockholder might take and keep the $40 cash dividends instead of the stock, yet, as it was so much less than the actual market value of the stock, it was an option of no value, and no prudent man would avail himself of it."

The judge ought to have added here, "Out of our

jurisdiction." But *within* our jurisdiction, Heaven save the mark! let the prudent man take what he can get, while he is in the way with his adversary, particularly if he is a *cestui que trust*, and the adversary is a trustee or a remainder-man. We'll show in a minute what these foolish daughters of Eve lost by not taking the cash — supposing they could have got it. The court admit that there was an implied option with the stockholders to take cash or stock, but insist that the option was of no value in this case, the stock being worth more than the cash. This means that $100 is of no value to a man who is entitled to a share of stock that is worth $163. But who will undertake to say that $100 in cash is not a good deal better than nothing? The court continue: —

> "If he did not wish to keep the stock, he would take it and sell. If he took the stock, it was not expected that he should first receive the $40 and then pay it back to the treasurer for the stock; for it is stated that the $280,000 were already invested in mills, machinery, and other property. Nor was any formality necessary on the part of the shareholder, except to assent to the transaction, and receive a certificate. By receiving a certificate, the substance of the transaction was that the shareholder received a stock dividend; and the substance of the transaction is to determine its character."

If the substance of this transaction were to determine its character, it would be disposed of very readily. The substance of it is that the directors intended to make a lawful dividend of net earnings, — such a dividend as directors are in the habit of making every year, and such a dividend as no chancellor or bench of judges speaking the English language ever before styled capital, or treated as capital, when the directors had styled it in words "dividend." The directors intended to make, and did make, a dividend *eo nomine;* and a dividend *eo nomine* "means" the same thing as income within our jurisdiction, and IS the same thing as income everywhere on the face of the earth, "out of our jurisdiction." This being the substance of the transaction thus far, this dividend belongs clearly to the beneficiaries of the dividends of this company. Now let us see what the judges do with it: —

> "No prudent trustee would doubt that he ought to elect to take the shares, having a market value of $163, rather than the dividend in cash; and, indeed, the defendants ask for a decree to that effect. They pray that the trustees may be directed not merely to take the money, but to pay it directly back to the treasurer and receive the new shares therefor, thereby obtaining a stock dividend. But, if the trustees receive it as a cash dividend, they are to credit it and account for it as cash. The stock would then remain in the hands of the company, and the remainder-men might receive their proportion of its value. This is not what the plaintiffs desire. *They ask, in substance, that the trustees shall take the stock, but shall pay it to the tenants for life as income.*"

What cormorants! Such grasping avarice might well enough excite the generous indignation of the court! We can see the judges peering over their spectacles at each other in mute amazement at the audacity of Mrs. Williams and her sisters. Where's Cruikshank! No other pencil than that of the immortal limner of Mr. Bumble and the Board, could do adequate justice to this scene. "Brother Colt, what is the world coming to? These good women are not content with the *money* their father left them, — we might manage to strain a point and give them *that*, — but they want all that the money will buy for them, and this is 'most tolerable and not to be endured.'" It's the old scene over again; the Board in solemn conclave, — beadle enters in excitement, — "'Mr. Limbkins, I beg your pardon, sir; Oliver Twist has asked for more.' There was a general start. Horror was depicted on every countenance. 'For *more!*' said Mr. Limbkins. 'Compose yourself, Bumble, and answer me distinctly. Do I understand that he asked for more, *after he had eaten the supper allowed by the dietary?*'"

But the ladies in this case have not eaten their supper, and the Supreme Judicial Dietary have decided that, in consequence of their ill-timed objections to the supper they might have had, they shall have no supper at all. They might have been entitled, possibly, to their forty per cent. in cash, but they come to the court to get stock which was more valuable, and the court decide that they can have neither cash nor stock, but that the trustee shall lay out the money in stock and keep it for the remainder-man! Read the *finale* of Mr. Justice Chapman's opinion: —

> "We think it clearly their duty to take the stock; but, being a stock dividend, they should treat it as capital. *Decree accordingly.*"

We observe here that the court do not venture to say that this dividend *is* capital, but merely that the trustees should "*treat it*" as capital. And why in heaven's name should the trustees "treat it" otherwise than as what it is? The court are usually somewhat guarded in their expressions when they meddle with this aspect of the matter. They "treat" it as capital; they "regard" it as capital; it is in the "nature" of capital, so that you would imagine it depended merely on the way you looked at it whether it was the one thing or the other. "*Fancy* it Burgundy," says the tapster of his ale; "fancy it Burgundy, — only fancy it, — and it 's worth ten shillings a quart." So say the judges of this dividend, substantially, — " Fancy it capital, — only fancy it, — and it 's as good capital as you 'll find in Massachusetts." And it is all fancy, this talk about the " nature " of capital, and this conversion of income into capital by " treating " and " regarding " it as capital.

We are, however. gratified in this opinion by a foreshadow of the policy of the court in regard to optional dividends. Those of my readers who have read the Layman's Review of *Minot* v. *Paine*, may remember a table from " Poor's Railroad Manual," introduced to illustrate the form and substance of the dividends made for a series of years by the Philadelphia and Reading Railroad Company. It will be convenient to reprint that table, the better to illustrate the position of the Supreme Judicial Court of Massachusetts on this interesting subject : —

DIVIDENDS OF THE PHILADELPHIA AND READING RAILROAD.

	Cash.	Stock.	Optional.
January, 1863		7	
December, 1863		7	
November, 1864		15	
December, 1865			10
July, 1866		5	
December, 1866			5
July, 1867	5		
January, 1868		5	
July, 1868		5	
January, 1869		5	
July, 1869		5	
January, 1870	5		
December, 1870	5		

With this table in view, it was asked of the court how it would apply the *Rule in Minot's case.* The eight stock dividends were capital. The three cash dividends were income. But we were at sea with regard to the two optional dividends. Let us show at first what the directors of the company made them, by annexing their advertisement: —

"PHILADELPHIA AND READING R. R. CO.
Office No. 227 South Front Street,
PHILAD., *Dec.* 11, 1865.

"DIVIDEND NOTICE. — The transfer books of this Company will be closed on Saturday, December 16, and reopened on Tuesday, January 9, 1866.

"A dividend of TEN PER CENT. has been declared on the preferred and common stock, clear of National and State taxes, payable in cash or common stock at par, at the option of the holder, on and after the 30th instant, to the holders thereof as they shall stand registered on the books of the Company on the 10th instant. All payable at this office. S. BRADFORD, *Treasurer.*"

It will be observed that this was a dividend *eo nomine*, so made by the power competent to declare dividends, and it was payable in cash or in common stock at par. If *Minot* v. *Paine* had been law in 1863, the beneficiary of a trust fund composed of Reading Railroad stock, would have been refused his dividends for 1863 and 1864 because they were made in stock, and yet the fifteen per cent. dividend was paid under the following advertisement: —

"*November* 30, 1864.

"DIVIDEND NOTICE. — A DIVIDEND of 15 PER CENT. on the common and preferred stock has been declared, payable in *common stock*, on 31st December to holders registered on 15th December."

But now comes an *optional* dividend of ten per cent. Here is a chance for the beneficiary. How is the trustee to take it, in cash or in stock? *Minot* v. *Paine* does not enlighten us. The supplementary decision in *Daland* v. *Williams*, solves the difficulty. If the stock is above par, a "prudent trustee" would be required by that decision to take the dividend in stock, and retain it for the remainder-man. Now Reading stock, when the dividend was announced, 11th December, 1865, was selling on the New York stock exchange at from $116.50 to $117.25. When the dividend was payable, 30th December, the stock sold, dividend off, at $106.75. Under the decision in *Daland* v. *Williams*, the "prudent trustee" would have been bound to take the stock. The holders were no doubt satisfied that the dividend was made from net earnings, so the stock fell only to the amount of the dividend, and the dividend was capital in view of Massachusetts law. If the stock had fallen below par, in consequence of a suspicion that the directors were making their dividends not from profits but from capital stock, then it would have been the duty of a "prudent trustee" to have taken cash instead of stock, and the cash would have been income to the *cestui que trust.* That is to say, when there is no reason to doubt that an optional dividend is made from earnings it is capital; when there is some reason to fear that it is a division of capital it becomes income. Indeed, under this decision, a dividend may be capital in the morning and income in the afternoon. It may shift its character half a dozen times a day, as the stock fluctuates on the exchange from 99 to 101.

But suppose the stock is at par! The $100 that is payable under an optional dividend, will purchase just $100 worth of shares. The trustee may take either. If he take cash it is income; if he take stock it is capital. He has no right to put such an interpretation on the law as will best consult the interests of the beneficiary. Then what is he to do in this dilemma? Make a case, — pay lawyers, — and go before Messrs. Chapman and Co., and ask what he can do with safety.

And what will Messrs. Chapman and Co. tell him? Perhaps they would tell him to divide, and give half to one and half to the other. If there is any law in *Minot* v. *Paine*, that would be the only way. But there can be no convenient compromise. The net earnings are either income or capital, — they can be one or the other, but they cannot be both; and, as they are represented *both* by stock and cash, it is impossible, under *Minot* v. *Paine*, to say what they are. The impossibility of settling what an optional dividend is, when the stock is at par, continues in spite of *Daland* v. *Williams*.

But there was another optional dividend in the Reading Table. The directors published a *Dividend Notice* in the premises, stating that they would pay, on the 31st of December, 1866, a *dividend* of five per cent. in cash or common stock at par. The option was to cease on 30th of March, after which the dividend was payable in cash only. The stock was above par on the settlement day, and under the doctrine of the Supreme Court the dividend would have been an accretion of capital for the remainder-man.

The result of the application of the simple rule to the Reading Table would have resulted as follows. In the seven years between 1863 and 1870, the beneficiary of Reading in trust would have received three semi-annual dividends of five per cent. *if they were made in the usual manner;* and the remainder-man would have secured six dividends of five per cent., two dividends of seven, one dividend of ten, and one dividend of fifteen. That is to say, the remainder-man would have secured fifty-nine per cent. increase upon the *corpus* that was never intended for him; and the real beneficiary of the income would have starved for seven years on the three five per cent. dividends. Is not this sheer robbery of the beneficiary, under color of law?

Now let us see the explanation of these stock dividends, as made by the directors, with the comment of the money-article of the "New York Tribune" for February 11, 1870:—

> "The Company negotiated at par five millions seven per cent. convertible bonds, and hereafter the earnings of the Company can be appropriated to the payment of semi-annual cash dividends. The report shows that $10,683,859 of aggregate *stock dividends* has been used as the representative of $17,592,258 of actual *net earnings* invested in permanent improvements, leaving in fact $6,913,399 of net earnings belonging to the stockholders, and for which they are entitled to stock dividends."

It is not worth while to waste a word of comment on this statement. It may be added, however, that since January, 1870, the dividends of the Reading have been made in cash.

In the "Review" of *Minot* v. *Paine*, I passed over, without sufficient consideration, the prior decisions of the Supreme Court of Massachusetts, which were supposed to have authorized or influenced it. It will be remembered that the Chief Justice claimed for his new rule that while it is more "in conformity with the legal and equitable rights of stockholders than any that has been suggested, it is also in conformity with the decisions of this court, as far as the subject has been considered." The persistence of the court in going, in *Daland* v. *Williams*, "further in the same direction" than it had gone in *Minot* v. *Paine*, induced me to look once more into the prior cases, with the view of ascertaining precisely to what extent they are in conformity with the new decisions. I find on more particular examination that, as far as they consider the same subject, the cases referred to *are not in conformity with Minot* v. *Paine in any respect whatever.*

The first of these cases is that of *Reed* v. *Head*, 6 Allen, 174. This case is a very important one, as showing what the court once understood by the words "dividend" and "income," and the length to which they were disposed to go in January, 1863, in maintaining the popular understanding of the terms. The court had not at that time absolutely abandoned the use of the English dictionary, but employed words according to their lexicographal meaning.

The head-note in this leading case will amuse all lawyers and amaze all laymen who are familiar with the *Rule in Minot's case.* It is in the following words:—

> "If a legacy is given of the DIVIDENDS OR INCOME upon stock in a land company, which is known to derive its profits from the improvement and sale of land, the legacy will include ALL DIVIDENDS which may be declared thereon, *although the same in reality consist of a portion of the capital stock of the company.*"

Thus you perceive in the case of a land company (which happened to be an incorporated water-power company), ALL DIVIDENDS, whether in *cash* or in *stock*, which may include scrip and land, "however large," and "however made," are income to the fortunate *cestui que trust* to whom the testator has devised them. That is to say, you may divide the *corpus*, but the dividend will go to the beneficiary of the income.

But it is not fair to quote only the head-note, because the six judges tell us that this decision is in "conformity "with that of *Minot* v. *Paine*, "so far as the subject has been considered." It is just, therefore, to give the

4

judges who decided the latter case the full benefit of the very language of the court.

"According to the fair interpretation of the will of Elizabeth Smith, the legacies of the Water Power and Mill Dam stock, which are the subject of this suit, are given in trust, the *dividends* to be paid to the legatees, during their lives; and after they are severally deceased the stock is devised over. The word 'dividend' is used in the legacy to Elizabeth Smith Head, and the word 'income' in the legacy to James E. Head; but *both obviously mean the same thing.*"

In view of subsequent cases the judicial determination that dividends are obviously the same thing as income, or more succinctly, that DIVIDENDS ARE OBVIOUSLY INCOME, becomes very interesting. But there is more of the same sort: —

" It appears that these corporations, which were originally formed with a view to make dividends out of the receipts for the use of water power, mills and tolls from the use of the mill-dam as a way, afterwards changed their purpose, and became land companies, and that since this change their dividends are made from the avails of the sales of the property which constitutes their capital stock. They are, therefore, dividing not merely their earnings, but their principal."

The court then allude to the English authorities in regard to extraordinary dividends, which the chancellors at one time held to be dividends above two and one half per cent. semi-annually on Bank of England stock, citing our old friends, *Brander* v. *Brander*, and *Paris* v. *Paris*. But these authorities the court put aside as inapplicable, for in this case they hold the dividends not extraordinary, although they are composed partly of capital. " It is true," they add, " that the whole capital stock may be exhausted by the dividends in the lifetime of the legatees for life; but on the other hand it is quite possible that a large sum will be left in remainder."

Now this is not only laying down a simple rule, but it is carrying the rule to the very extreme. *Dividends are obviously income even though they may exhaust the whole capital stock.* We were inclined to think this too far, perhaps, for a court of equity to go in this direction; but on reflection, we could not tell where they could stop short of it on solid ground. And when we saw that this decision was concurred in by Bigelow, Dewey, Metcalf and Merrick, as well as by Hoar and Chapman, we were satisfied that it was law, and were surprised to find that the opinion of the court was delivered by the same gentleman who was their mouthpiece in *Minot* v. *Paine.* There was such a world of space between the proposition of 1863 — *dividends including capital income* — and the proposition of 1868 — *dividends of net earnings capital* — that it was difficult to imagine how any man could have committed himself to both of them, unless he possessed a remarkable facility for becoming the conduit of other people's opinions, without having any opinion of his own. I wonder if Theron Metcalf — who is as clear and accurate in his use of language, as he is reputed to be profound in the knowledge of the law — would undertake to bridge over the chasm between these two decisions, so as to afford a safe passage from the one to the other for the young gentlemen who have succeeded him.

But there is another case in which this subject has been considered. *Atkins* v. *Albree*, 12 Allen, 359, is also claimed to be in conformity with *Minot* v. *Paine.* In this case the income of twenty shares of the Boston Gas Light Company, devised to trustees, was left to Mrs. Albree by the will of her husband, remainder over to his nephew. The company wished to increase their business, and determined to increase their capital stock by the issue of five hundred new shares of the value of $500 each, which sum was to be assessed on them and paid by the stockholders in the proportion of one share of new stock to four shares of old. It was not a dividend of profits or net earnings, either in fact or in name. There is no reason to suppose from the report that there was any accumulation of gains from which these shares were created, or from which any extra dividends could have been declared. The new stock was to be issued and assessed, and the directors were authorized to sell all new shares not taken by a certain date, and pay over the premium (if any) derived from them to the parties entitled to the right of subscribing for them. In the absence of any statement to that effect, the court could not have considered the right to subscribe for these new shares as gain, revenue, produce, proceeds, profits or receipts from the existing shares.

The trustees had no money to invest in the new shares, so the rights were sold for $1373.95, which was claimed *in presenti* both by the remainder-man and the *cestui que trust.* The court decided that it belonged to neither, but *to the fund;* and so decided, expressly on the ground that it was *not gain or income actually earned by the corporation.*

We find nothing in this decision to criticize, because we find nothing in it in conformity with *Minot* v. *Paine.* It does not say that lawful dividends of net earnings may not be made in rights to take stock, or in stock itself, as well as in greenbacks or in gold. It does not say that where directors declare a dividend *eo nomine*, regular or extraordinary, it should not be held income unless it were a dividend of cash. On the contrary, it leaves us to infer that if the premium which the rights brought had been the result of net gain or income actually earned by the corporation, it would have been adjudged to the *cestui que trust.* The Boston Gas Company says by its directors: "We are doing a good business, and can increase it to advantage if we can procure more capital, but we have no accumulated earnings, and must assess our new capital at par on the stockholders." Here there is nothing whatever to which the beneficiary of the income can lay claim; and whether the stock thus subscribed for is worth what it costs, or twenty-five per cent. above cost, is a matter in which he has no concern. But this lies so entirely within the discretion of the directors that if they had said, without any explanation, "We hereby declare a *dividend* of twenty-five per cent., payable in rights to subscribe to new shares" — in certain proportions, — there is nothing in the language of Chief Justice Bigelow to lead us to suppose that he would have held such dividend capital, even if it had been shown not to consist of net earnings. He would not have gone behind the resolution of the directors to ascertain of what the dividend was composed.

It must not be forgotten that when Chief Justice Bigelow said that the value of the right to subscribe for new shares must be regarded as a part of the *corpus* of the property devised, he was speaking of the naked right to participate in the creation of new stock, — the same question in fact that was decided in *Gray* v. *Portland Bank*, 3 Mass. 364. In that case a bank incorporated with the privilege of creating a stock not less than a sum certain, and of increasing that stock to another sum, commenced business on the smaller capital, and afterwards increased it to the larger. It was decided by the court that those who held the stock in the capital first raised had a right to subscribe for and hold the new stock in proportion to their respective shares. In this case the new stock derived perhaps additional value from the fact that the directors had a reserved fund of profits which they had not seen fit to divide, and until dividend declared no question could arise as to its beneficiary. The same is true of *Atkins* v. *Albree.* But another and a very different state of things arises, when profits are intended to be divided, and dividends are declared, in shares, or rights to shares, or scrip, or notes of hand, or bonds, or anything else that is money's worth and may be converted into cash. When the Portland Bank increased their $100,000 capital to $200,000, and Mr. Gray claimed the right to duplicate his seventy shares, there was no DIVIDEND involved in the case. It would have been absurd to call it a dividend, because the surplus that was supposed to give the value to the new shares was *reserved, and not divided.* When the Boston Gas Light Company voted to increase their capital stock by the addition of $250,000, which the directors agreed to assess on the stockholders in a certain proportion, there may have been a surplus profit that made the new shares above par from the start; but that value depended on the fact that this surplus (if any) had been *reserved, and not divided.* Instead of a dividend, there was merely an assessment, and it is not worth while to claim a dividend until there comes to be a division. But when the *division of profits* comes, then the right of the tenant for life is fixed; and before *Minot* v. *Paine* he knew that the dividend declared was his income. Whether or not his dividend is his income, is now something that he must consult the court about, or the decisions "not yet reported;" though it has always been held, even in England, that everything given in terms as a DIVIDEND belongs to the tenant for life and not to the remainder man.

In *Paris* v. *Paris*, 10 Ves. 185, an extraordinary division of a sum of money by the Bank of England among the proprietors of bank stock, beyond the usual dividend, was considered as capital, and therefore not the absolute property of the tenant for life; the Lord Chancellor (Eldon) following, but disapproving the former decisions, and adding: "It is true, the bank have it in their power to give the *bonus* to the tenant for life or not." That is by declaring an increased DIVIDEND.

In *Witts* v. *Steere* a *bonus* was held capital, the Lord Chancellor (Erskine) observing, however, that the bank might avoid the question altogether, — "for they may increase the DIVIDEND," — as there was no doubt that the increased *dividend* would belong to the tenant for life.

In *Hooper* v. *Rossiter*, 13 Price, 778, the Lord Chief Baron (Alexander) held the following language: "It seems to have become an established principle, as the result deducible from all the cases (and I have considered them carefully), that where the increase can be *shown* to be a DIVIDEND, the tenant for life is to have it, but where it cannot be so considered, it must be taken as an accretion of capital, and then it must necessarily go to the remainder-man." In this case the question arose on "apportionment" of newly created stock among the "proprietors" as "capital," *eo nomine*. Even in that case the Chief Baron admitted that he yielded reluctantly to the pressure of *Brander* v. *Brander*, and the cases in the same line.

It is clear from these cases that in England, as long ago as 1824, there was a disposition to treat *bonuses* as income; and that from the earliest cases cited there was no question that what directors chose to make DIVIDEND was always considered dividend by the courts. But the later cases go still further. In *Johnson* v. *Johnson*, 15 Jur. 714 (1850), a "*bonus* or increased dividend of £10 per share .was added to the usual dividend of £3 per share, making altogether £13 per share." According to the old doctrine which worried Erskine, such a dividend would have been what he pronounced it in *Witts* v. *Steere*, under the pressure of our old friend *Brander* v. *Brander*. But now Knight Bruce, V. C., says, "I consider this *bonus* to be income."

So in *Murray* v. *Glasse*, 17 Jur. 816 (1853), the Vice-Chancellor (Wood) says: "The widow is entitled to have all the dividends accrued due on the Mint shares since the testator's decease, *and the bonuses also if they were paid out of profits*."

In *Plumb* v. *Neild*, 6 Jur. (N. S.) 529 (1860), a banking company out of the net profits of the half year declared a dividend, and also paid a sum of money on each share which they called a *bonus;* it was held, that the *bonus* was income and not capital as between the tenant for life and the remainder-man. The Vice Chancellor (Kindersley) seemed to think that the right of the tenant to a dividend of profits could not be affected by "calling it bonus."

In *Ward* v. *Combe*, 7 Sim. R. 634 (1836), the Vice-Chancellor (Shadwell) gave the summary of the doctrine on this point in the following words: "The cases amount to this: that *if the increase is given by way of dividend, it must be taken as such*."

The same Vice-Chancellor, some years afterwards, in *Price* v. *Anderson*, 15 Sim. R. 477 (1847), said most emphatically that the case was very plain, and that the question must be determined by the mode in which "the *company* have dealt with their profits." The company, he said, if they had seen fit might have declared that a portion of their distributed profits should be capital and a part dividend, but inasmuch as they had *declared* the whole to be *dividend*, "THEREFORE the tenant for life is entitled to the whole."

So far the English cases. But the true doctrine with regard to dividend is stated with equal force and directness in the opinion of Judge James, of the Supreme Court of New York, in the case of *Clarkson* v. *Clarkson*, 18 Bar. 646. And by the way, unlike Turveydrop, this judge does not stand on the "manner" of payment, which he says is a mere matter of policy with the company. Nor does he undertake to put directors under guardianship, or to overrule Webster's Dictionary.

"'Dividends,' as used in the will, is unqualified; it includes in its technical sense, as well as in its ordinary and common acceptation, *all distribution to corporators, of the profits of the corporation*, whether such distributions are large or small; or whether made at long or at short intervals; and *without any regard to the manner or place of their declaration, or mode of payment.* The testator is presumed to have used words in their natural and primary sense; and from the terms used, in his will, it is clear that he intended that all the gains, profits, income, and proceeds of the two shares of his estate, of whatsoever name or nature, should go to his daughters, as tenants for life; and that intention should not be defeated."

These cases are cited to illustrate the doctrine that the declaration of the directors determines absolutely the question of dividend; and that the Supreme Judicial Court of Massachusetts were in an unusual state of legal inspiration when they recognized in *Reed* v. *Head* this universal truth, and laid down the short, simple, and sufficient rule — "THE WORD DIVIDEND · · AND THE WORD INCOME, · · · BOTH OBVIOUSLY MEAN THE SAME THING." There is *terra-firma*, hard-pan, adamant. *There* is a rule that every testator and every trustee might be made to comprehend, and that does not require to be "modified" more or less at every term of the court. Instead of being such a rule, that the more you take away from it the better you make it, it admits of no exception and requires no qualification. The court might have expressed it in fewer words: thus, "*Dividends mean Income*," — though it matters little what "Dividends *mean*" as long as judges can make what they please of them by merely "regarding," "considering," or "treating" them as something else, in which case (judicially speaking) they inevitably "accrue" precisely as may be desired, without any reference whatever to their meaning. The fact that they are thus made what they are not is only a "patent objection" — not fit to influence the "perverted" minds of gentlemen on a Bench, superior naturally and by education to "patent objections," though open sometimes to "considerations of a legal character," — "in decisions not yet reported."

BOSTON, *May Day*, 1871.

THE END.

www.ingramcontent.com/pod-product-compliance
Lightning Source LLC
LaVergne TN
LVHW011128110826
845150LV00008B/2275

* 9 7 8 1 4 1 8 1 9 4 9 6 3 *